G[ROW...]

Understanding The Step By Step Approach To Planting, Maintaining, Harvesting Banana For Beginners

BLADE JAVION

Table of Contents

INTRODUCTORY

Bananas are grown commercially for their fruit, which is known as banana cultivation, banana farming, or banana horticulture. Bananas are grown in tropical and subtropical climates all over the world and are one of the world's most popular fruits. They are a good source of fibre, potassium, and vitamin C in addition to being delicious.

Learn the basics of banana farming by reading this:

• Bananas require warm, moist soil and an average annual temperature of 20 to 35 degrees Celsius (68 to 95 degrees Fahrenheit) in order to grow successfully. They need a lot of sunshine and consistent rainfall, preferably between 2,000 and 2,500 millimetres (80 and 100 inches) every year. Loamy soil with a high water-holding capacity is great for growing bananas.

• Bananas can be grown from a wide range of different types, each with its own set of desirable qualities. Cavendish, Grand Nain (Chiquita Banana), Lady Finger (Sugar Banana), and Plantain are some of the more well-known types. Varieties are selected based on a number of criteria, including market demand, disease resistance, and environmental characteristics in the area.

• Preparing the soil is essential before planting anything. This process entails removing any obstacles, such weeds or debris, before plowing the soil to break it up and add organic material like compost to boost fertility.

• Growing new plants from the mother plant is called "suckering," and it is the most common method of asexual propagation for bananas. A fresh crop can be started by carefully removing suckers from the mother plant and replanting them. Banana plantlets free of disease are mass-produced using tissue culture propagation methods.

• When planting banana trees, make sure to leave enough room between each plant for it to flourish. Plants should be spaced 2–3 meters (6–10 feet) apart in a row, and rows should be spaced 3–4 meters (10–13 feet) apart. It's important to dig a hole that's big enough for the plant's roots.

• Taking good care of banana plants is crucial if you want to have a successful yield. Maintaining healthy plants requires consistent watering, mulching to keep moisture in the soil, and feeding plants with the right fertilizers. Weeding, insect management, and using supports for particularly heavy clusters are all essential parts of plant upkeep.

• Bananas have a wide range of harvest times because it all depends on the cultivar. From planting to the first harvest, it usually takes roughly 9-12 months. Bananas are often picked when they are ripe but still have their green color. Bunches are harvested from the plant and handled gently to prevent bruising.

• Bananas are transported to packing facilities after harvest where they are cleaned, sorted, and packed for distribution. Bananas are perishable and need to be stored in ideal conditions to keep their freshness and increase their shelf life.

In the right climate, growing bananas may be a lucrative business. However, success calls for an understanding of disease management, crop rotation, and market dynamics. Those considering starting a banana farm can benefit greatly from consulting with local agricultural extension services and seasoned banana farmers.

CHAPTER ONE
Bananas Features

There are many different kinds of bananas, each with its own special qualities and flavour. Some of the most well-liked bananas are listed below.

• Bananas of the Cavendish kind are the most extensively grown and consumed type around the world. They have a creamy, sweet flavour and turn a bright yellow colour when ripe. The Cavendish kind of banana is the most widely available in grocery stores and is typically used for fresh eating.

• Banana relative plantain is more often used in cooking than eaten fresh. They differ from dessert bananas in that they are larger and more starchy. Green plantains are unripe, and they ripen to a yellow or black colour. They are a staple in many tropical cuisines and are often prepared by frying, boiling, or baking.

• Lady Finger (Sugar Banana): Smaller and sweeter than a regular Cavendish banana, Lady Finger bananas are also known as Sugar Bananas or Pisang Raja. They're quite tasty and smooth in texture. Bananas cut into thin "fingers" are a common ingredient in many sweets, drinks, and snacks.

• Red bananas are smaller than Cavendish bananas and have a reddish-purple skin when ripe. They are deliciously sweet and smooth in texture. Red bananas are a popular ingredient in baked goods, salads, and as a decorative accent.

• Bananas from the Blue Java variety are commonly referred to as "ice cream bananas" due to their unusual flavour and creamy texture. When unripe, their skin has a blue green colour, but once ripe, it turns a bright yellow. Bananas from the Blue Java variety can be utilized in a wide range of culinary contexts.

• Apple bananas, also known as Manzano bananas, are exceptionally sweet and taste like a cross between an apple and a strawberry. When ripe, their yellow skin is speckled with black dots, making them easily distinguishable from regular Cavendish bananas, which are shorter and thinner. Banana apples are versatile and can be utilized in a variety of sweet applications.

• Burro Bananas are medium-sized bananas that are thick, short, and blocky in appearance. When unripe, they are a dull yellow with green tips, and when mature, they turn a brighter yellow with black specks. Burro bananas are utilized in both savoury and sweet preparations due to their acidic and lemony taste.

• Disease resistance is one of the many benefits of the Goldfinger banana, a newer cultivar. These bananas look like Cavendish bananas but have a much more delicate skin. Goldfinger bananas are utilized both fresh and cooked due to their creamy texture and mild sweetness.

There are many different kinds of bananas, and these are just a few examples. It's possible that there are regionally distinct variants in existence. Factors including personal preference, culinary application, market demand, and regional growing circumstances all play a role in determining which banana variety to plant.

The Economic Importance Of Banana Farming

There are many parts of the world where growing bananas is crucial to the local economy. Here are some of the most important reasons why growing bananas is so important financially:

• Since growing bananas requires a lot of manual labour, it can be used to create a lot of jobs. Banana growing requires labourers at every stage of the supply chain, from pre-production planning to post-harvest cleaning. Farmers, agricultural labourers, and locals all benefit from this since it increases their ability to make a living.

• Money in the Bank Bananas are a popular and profitable fruit around the world. The commercial production of bananas has the potential to be a highly profitable venture. Farmers can sell their produce at neighbourhood fairs, wholesale markets, retail stores, and international trade shows to generate cash. Banana cultivation is important to the economies of the countries and regions where it is practised because of the money it brings in.

• Export Possibilities: Bananas are a major source of revenue for many banana-producing countries. Banana exports provide these countries with a means to compete economically on a global scale. Banana exports are a key source of cash for countries like Ecuador, the Philippines, Costa Rica, Colombia, and Honduras.

• The banana business has a robust value chain that generates employment opportunities in several areas, including transportation, packing, storage, distribution, and marketing. Truck drivers, packers, quality inspectors, warehouse employees, and salespeople are just a few examples of the diverse workforce spawned by the various links in the value chain. Beyond just basic production, the banana value chain helps to generate income and employment opportunities.

• Banana farming is essential for smallholder farmers since it provides them with a sustainable means of income and food security. Bananas can be grown profitably on relatively small areas of land by small-scale farmers who then sell their fruit either locally or to larger producers and exporters. Small farmers can enhance their incomes and get access to commercial agriculture markets by growing bananas.

• Especially in areas where agriculture is the predominant economic activity, banana production is crucial to rural development. The money from growing bananas stays in rural areas, helping to finance and improve things like shops, clinics, and roads. It helps alleviate poverty and raises living conditions for people in rural areas.

• Banana farming allows farmers to diversify their income streams by engaging in other sectors of the food production industry. Farmers can lessen the dangers of mono-cropping and reliance on a single crop by including bananas in their crop rotation or farming techniques. The economic and environmental stability of farms can be improved by diversification.

Growing bananas has a major impact on economies at all levels, from the level of individual farmers and rural communities to that of entire nations. It should be kept in mind, however, that obstacles like market fluctuations, diseases, climate change, and trade policies can all have a negative effect on the profitability of growing bananas. To ensure the long-term economic viability of the banana sector, sustainable farming techniques, research and development, and enabling policies are all necessary.

CHAPTER TWO
Botanical Taxonomy And Structure

Classification of Plants:

Bananas are members of the genus Musa in the family Musaceae. Various species and hybrids exist within the Musa genus. Musa acuminata, best known for its delicious dessert bananas, is the most widely produced species. Musa balbisiana, a different species, is used for culinary and plantain uses.

A Banana Tree's Internal Structure:

There are several parts that make up a banana plant.

• The rhizome is the plant's underground stem from which new bananas grow. New banana plants begin as shoots, or suckers, that emerge from the rhizome and eventually mature.

• The pseudostem is the part of the banana plant that is visible above ground and is made up of overlapping leaf sheaths. The cylindrical shape of the pseudostem is a result of the protective sheaths that surround it.

• Banana leaves are quite broad and massive, emerging from the pseudostem. The leaves are tall and narrow, with a prominent midvein and parallel side veins. They grow in a

24

spiral pattern and can reach lengths of several meters.

• Banana fruit begins as an inflorescence, the flowering structure of the banana plant. A big cluster, known as a bunch or a hand, arises from the pseudostem's middle. Each of the blossoms in the layered bunch will eventually turn into its own banana.

• The fruit of the banana tree is the most widely consumed edible portion of the plant. It's a berry with a juicy, velvety interior and a tough outer skin. The size, colour, and taste of banana fruits might change depending on the variety. Fruits of cultivated species are often elongated and curved, and they contain seeds, albeit ones that are small and immature.

• The fibrous roots of banana plants help them draw moisture and nutrients up from the earth. The plant's roots provide it strength and steadiness.

Banana plants can differ slightly in anatomy according on species, variety, and growth stage. The above is a high-level summary of the fundamental parts of a normal banana plant.

Lifestyle And Patterns Of Development

Bananas are notable for their peculiar development patterns and multi-staged life cycle. The growth and development of a banana plant are summarized below:

• Bananas can generate offspring asexually by forming and planting suckers, which are new shoots that grow from the rhizome. To start new banana plants, these "suckers" are cut from the mother plant. Banana plants can be multiplied quickly using this strategy.

• Banana plants, after being planted, go through a phase of vegetative growth. New leaves develop from the plant's core and the pseudostem becomes longer. The plant puts all of its energy into producing a strong root system and a dense canopy of leaves.

• Inducing Flowering: Age, Environmental Conditions, and Cultural Practices Influence Banana Plants' Transition from Vegetative Growth to Flowering. Inducing flowering typically occurs after 9–15 months of growth, though this varies greatly by species and environmental factors.

• Once the banana plant begins to bloom, a flower-bearing structure called an inflorescence develops at the very end of the pseudostem. The inflorescence emerges and expands fast, producing clusters or hands of flowers. Depending on the cultivar, the inflorescence's development can span multiple months.

• The process of flowering and fruit formation begins when an inflorescence's individual flowers are pollinated and fertilized. The flowers die off and the ovaries develop into fruit when fertilization is successful. The fruit swells in size as additional hands or layers of fruit form on the inflorescence.

• The process of ripening and harvesting results in a change in colour and biochemical composition of the fruit. Bananas are picked while they are fully mature but still green because they continue to ripen in storage.

Variety, end use, and consumer demand all play a role in determining the optimal time for harvest. After being picked, the bananas are left to mature until they are ready for sale or shipment.

• Banana plants often senesce, or die back, after fruiting, before regenerating the next year. When the fruit-bearing pseudostem begins to wither and die, it is a sign that the plant's life cycle has come to an end.

New suckers or shoots arise from the rhizome, however, during the growing phase, guaranteeing the plant's perpetual regeneration and survival.

It's worth noting that different banana varieties, growing conditions, and even farmer traditions can all affect when and for how long each stage of the plant's life cycle lasts. To promote healthy growth and optimize fruit output, proper management measures including as irrigation, fertilization, pest control, and disease management are essential throughout.

CHAPTER THREE
Techniques For Propagation And Reproduction

Although sexual reproduction may occur in some wild banana species, asexual reproduction is the norm for this plant. Bananas are propagated primarily through the following means:

1. Bananas are propagated most frequently by means of suckers. Suckers are new shoots that develop from a plant's rhizome. To propagate new banana trees, these cuttings are removed from the mother plant and replanted. There are three distinct sorts of suckers:

• Sword suckers are robust suckers that have formed into a pseudostem and have established a strong root system. Sword suckers are great for starting new plants from seed quickly and can be planted directly.

• Smaller suckers that haven't had a chance to grow a pseudostem and root system are called "water suckers." Their common name comes from the fact that you can simply submerge their stems in water to grow new plants. Water suckers can be put in the ground once they have established root systems.

• Maiden suckers are very little shoots that develop from the base of a plant

33

but lack a pseudostem and roots. They are typically taken from their parents and nurtured in a nursery until a pseudostem and root system have formed. When the young suckers are ready, they are placed in the ground.

2. Tissue culture is a cutting-edge technique for rapid banana reproduction. Banana tissue, such as shoot tips or meristems, are cultured in a nutrient-rich media in order to grow into disease-free plantlets that may be planted in the wild. Plants of uniform appearance and reliable quality can be grown in large quantities using tissue culture. After the seedlings have flourished in the lab, they are ready to be hardened off and planted in the ground.

• Bananas can be propagated by a variety of methods, but division isn't one of them. In order to propagate a mature banana plant, its rhizome must be cut into smaller pieces. These pieces are then used to start fresh banana plants from scratch. Wild banana species, especially those cultivated for specialized goals like breeding or study, are the ones that typically undergo division.

• Although most bananas are grown from cuttings, it is feasible to grow new plants from seeds of certain wild varieties. However, most commercial banana varieties are bred to produce few or no seeds. It is possible to harvest, clean, and propagate the seeds of wild banana kinds to grow new trees.

However, because to the inconsistency of seedlings and the lengthy period required for their development, this technique is less frequent in commercial banana farming.

It's important to remember that there are pros and downsides to every type of propagation. The ease of usage and reproducibility in plant genetics made possible by suckers have led to their widespread adoption. While tissue culture yields disease-free plants and allows for mass production, both are dependent on the availability of specialized facilities and knowledgeable personnel. The goals of the garden, the materials at hand, and the desired qualities in the offspring all play a role in deciding which method of propagation to choose.

Conditions Of Climate And Soil

Growing bananas successfully calls for a particular kind of weather and soil. Here are the most important things to think about:

Conditions in the Atmosphere:

• Bananas prefer warm, humid, and subtropical environments. Bananas thrive in temperatures between 25 and 30 degrees Celsius (77 and 86 degrees Fahrenheit). Growth is greatly slowed by temperatures below 14°C (57°F), whereas heat stress is caused by temperatures above 40°C (104°F) and might impact fruit development.

• Bananas need a lot of rain or constant irrigation throughout the year. Annual precipitation of 1,500–2,500 millimetres (59–98 inches) is ideal. However, with supplemental watering, they may survive on significantly lesser rainfall. Plant growth, fruit development, and the avoidance of water stress are all dependent on a steady supply of water.

• Bananas thrive in humid environments with a relative humidity of 60% to 80%. Humidity encourages leaf development and limits transpiration. Dense foliage can be a breeding ground for diseases, but proper ventilation can help keep things healthy.

• Bananas can't develop or bear fruit properly unless they get plenty of sun.

They do best in climates where there are a minimum of six to eight hours of sunlight per day. Weak plants and delayed fruiting can result from a lack of sunlight.

Prerequisites for Soil:

1. Bananas require soils that can hold a lot of water but still drain efficiently. The best soils for growing bananas are sandy loams and loamy soils. These soils drain well while yet holding on to enough water that plants can use it. Soils high in heavy clay tend to hold too much water, which can cause root rot.

• Bananas do best when grown in soil with a pH of 5.5 to 7.0. Soils with a slight acidity are ideal for these plants. When soil pH falls outside of this sweet spot, plants may not be able to fully take advantage of the nutrients they have access to.

• Bananas do best in soils with a high organic matter content and plenty of fertility. Soil with a higher concentration of organic matter has better structure, holds more water, and is more fertile. Organic material, such as compost or well-rotted manure, should be worked into the soil prior to planting.

• Banana plants require well-drained soil in order to thrive. Root rot and other illnesses can be caused by soggy or poorly drained soils. Waterlogging can be avoided with the use of contouring, raised beds, or drainage ditches if the soil's natural drainage is inadequate.

It's worth noting that different banana types may have varying sensitivity to temperature and moisture levels. Bananas don't always grow well no matter where they're planted because of factors including altitude, wind direction, and microclimates.

The specific climate and soil requirements for successful banana growth in a location can be learned by consulting with local agricultural specialists or extension agencies.

CHAPTER FOUR
Choosing And Preparing Seeds And Potted Plants

For successful banana growing, careful attention must be paid to the selection and preparation of planting material. The most important factors are as follows:

Planting Medium Choice:

1. Consider the following before choosing suckers for planting:

• To ensure a healthy root system and robust pseudostem, select larger suckers. One meter (three feet) is the bare minimum height requirement.

• Pest-Free: Make sure there are no pests or diseases in the suckers. If you want to keep your new plants disease-free, you need to start with healthy suckers.

• Choose a banana variety that will do well in the market, will thrive in your region, and will be put to good use in your kitchen.

• Suckers that are between 4 and 6 months old are typically the best choice. They are mature enough now to successfully establish themselves in their chosen field.

2. When deciding whether or not to use plantlets grown in a tissue culture setting, keep the following in mind:

• It's important to get your plantlets from a reliable nursery or tissue culture facility to make sure they're healthy.

• Certification: Verify that the plant cuttings have been given the all-clear from any applicable agencies or organizations.

• Plantlets grown in a greenhouse or other controlled environment must be acclimatized to outdoor conditions before being planted. This is done by gradually increasing the amount of time they spend in direct sunlight and decreasing the amount of time they spend in humid conditions.

Cleaning and Preparing Seeds and Plants:

1. Poor Victims:

• Carefully cut the suckers away from the parent plant, but keep the corm (rhizome) and roots connected.

• Reduce the sucker's transpiration loss by cutting down its leaves. For maximum photosynthesis, keep the top couple of leaves.

• The cut ends of the suckers should be dipped in a fungicide solution for disease prevention.

• To keep the treated suckers from drying out before planting, store them in a cool, damp location out of direct sunlight.

2. Preparing Plant Clones for Tissue Culture:

• The plantlets must be hardened off by gradually exposing them to outdoor circumstances, first in a controlled environment and then in the field. This aids the seedlings in adjusting to the new environmental conditions.

• When relocating your plant cuttings from the lab to their final containers, be sure to choose a potting mix that is both well-drained and has a high water-holding capacity.

• Care for the plantlets by giving them plenty of water and fertilizer during their acclimation period.

• Careful handling of the suckers or plantlets is necessary regardless of the planting medium to prevent damage or stress. Keep them in a cool, dark place out of the direct sunlight and away from the rain until you're ready to plant.

Selecting healthy suckers or certified plantlets and preparing them properly are crucial first steps toward establishing a solid basis for successful banana cultivation. Banana plants can be kept healthy and productive by following these steps that reduce the likelihood of pests, illnesses, and stunted development.

Managing Fields And Planting

The development and growth of banana plants depend heavily on planting and field management procedures. An outline of the process is as follows:

1. Choosing a Location:

• Determine the soil's fertility, pH, and nutrient concentration through a soil analysis. Beneficial recommendations for soil amendments and fertilizers can be made with this data in hand.

• Waterlogging can be avoided by either choosing a location with adequate natural drainage or by installing artificial drainage systems.

• To ensure optimal plant development and harvest yields, select a site that receives direct sunlight all day long.

2. Planting:

• Prepare planting holes that are big enough to house the suckers' or plantlets' root systems. The hole needs to be about 30 cm (12 inches) in width and depth.

• Keep plants spaced far enough apart to ensure optimal air circulation and light penetration. Plants should be spaced 2–4 meters (6–13 feet) apart, and rows should be spaced 3–4 meters (10–13 feet) apart; however, this varies by banana variety.

• The depth at which you put your suckers or plantlets should be the same as the soil in your nursery or bag. To account for settling, the soil level should be raised to just above the surrounding ground.

• To facilitate proper soil contact and root establishment, water the planting hole before inserting the sucker or plantlet.

3. Field Administration:

• Maintaining proper soil moisture levels, especially during dry seasons, requires consistent and ample watering. Don't overwater, as this might cause the soil to become soggy and the roots to rot.

• Mulching: Spread a layer of organic mulch (such as straw or dried leaves) over the plants' bases to keep the soil moist, prevent weeds from growing, and maintain a consistent temperature in the soil.

• Bananas have very specific nutrient needs, so it's important to use balanced fertilizers that meet those needs. Potassium (K) and nitrogen (N) rich fertilizers are essential for maximum development and harvest yields.

• Banana plants need consistent access to nutrients, water, and sunshine; weeds should be regularly removed from the planting area. If necessary, use herbicides in addition to mechanical or manual approaches.

• By doing regular pruning, you can keep your plant healthy by allowing it to breathe and reducing the likelihood of fungal illnesses. To keep each clump with just the right amount of plants, remove any suckers that sprout up.

• Pest and Disease Management Be on the lookout for pests and diseases on your plants on a consistent basis. To effectively manage pest and disease outbreaks, implement integrated pest management (IPM) approaches. These may include cultural, biological, and chemical control methods.

• Stability and Safety: Anchor your plants with stakes or trellises to keep them from tottering in the wind.

4. Harvesting:

• Bananas should be picked when they have attained optimal ripeness. This could be different for green, ripe, or processed varieties.

• Cut the bunches using a sharp knife or machete, leaving some of the pseudostem connected to the bunch to prevent the fruit from being damaged during transport.

• Bananas are often damaged by rough handling, so use caution after harvesting. The fruit needs to be sorted and graded according to size, colour, and quality. Fruit quality and storage life can be preserved through careful post-harvest management practices like correct packaging, cooling, and transport.

CHAPTER FIVE
Controlling Fertilizer And Food Supply

Banana plants require careful control of their nutrients and fertilizers in order to thrive and produce at their full potential. Here are the most important factors to think about:

1. Before you plant anything, it's a good idea to have your soil tested to see what nutrients it has and what pH level it's at. This examination aids in determining which nutrients are lacking or imbalanced so that correct fertilizer may be recommended.

2. Bananas have particular needs when it comes to macronutrients.

Banana plants mostly need the following macronutrients:

• Nitrogen (N): Nitrogen stimulates the development of plant leaves and stems. Nitrogen fertilizers should be applied in two parts: the first at the beginning of the growing season, and the second at the height of the growing season.

• Phosphorus (P): Root growth and blooming depend on phosphorus. Phosphorus fertilizers should be used both at planting and during the growing season.

• Potassium (K) is essential for a healthy plant and the growth and quality of its fruit. Use potassium fertilizers consistently, but especially while the plant is bearing fruit.

3. Banana plants need specific micronutrients as well for optimal growth. They are called micronutrients, and they consist of elements like iron (Fe), manganese (Mn), zinc (Zn), copper (Cu), boron (B), and molybdenum (Mo).

Soil micronutrient deficits are very uncommon, but they do develop in some places and under some circumstances. Soil testing or the presence of obvious symptoms can reveal micronutrient deficiency, at which point the correct micronutrient fertilizers can be applied.

4. Compost or well-rotted manure are two examples of organic matter that can be worked into the soil before planting to increase its fertility and nutrient availability. Structure, moisture, and nutrient retention in soil are all improved by the presence of organic matter.

5. Use of Fertilizers:

• The timing of fertilizer applications should be staggered so that plants have access to nutrients at all stages of growth. Use fertilizers in the lead-up to planting, during the growing and fruiting phases, and after harvest.

• Avoid getting fertilizer on the pseudostem or roots by applying it evenly around the base of the plant.

• Rates: Use the rates suggested by soil testing and your county's agricultural extension service. Rates should be adjusted according to plant development, fruiting, and the presence of obvious signs of nutrient insufficiency.

6. Effective nitrogen uptake by banana plants is dependent on careful regulation of irrigation. The availability of adequate moisture in the root zone guarantees that nutrients may be taken up and transported to the plant. Waterlogging or overwatering can cause nutrients to seep out or rot at the roots.

7. In addition to applying fertilizer to the soil, foliar fertilization can be used to boost nutrient uptake by the plant's leaves. Nutrient-rich foliar sprays can be used to correct either long-term nutrient imbalances or short-term deficits.

8. Constantly check your plants for signs of nutrient deficiency or excess, including yellowing leaves, stunted growth, or leaf burn, so you can make the necessary adjustments. Fertilizer doses should be modified in response to plant growth and soil nutrient status.

It's worth noting that fertilizer needs can change depending on factors including the banana variety, the soil, the climate, and the location. Experts in agriculture or extension services in your area can advise you on the best methods for fertilizer management in your region.

Banana plants acquire the nutrients they need for powerful development, abundant fruit output, and overall plant vitality thanks to careful nutrition and fertilizer management.

Methods Of Pruning And Conditioning

Banana plants benefit greatly from proper pruning and training, which also increases their yield of fruit and eases the burden of management. Some common methods for shaping and shaping up banana plants are as follows:

1. Sucker Extraction:

• Only one primary sucker should be allowed to develop per plant. After the parent plant bears fruit, this sucker will take its place.

• All secondary suckers should be cut off at the base of the plant. These shoots, known as suckers, compete with the parent plant for resources, lowering the plant's total output.

• The underground water suckers (water suckers) must be cut off at the rhizome. These shoots take resources away from the mother plant.

2. Leaf Control:

• Banana trees lose their lower, less productive leaves as they age, so it's important to prune them regularly. Regularly removing dead, yellowed, or otherwise damaged leaves helps keep the plant healthy and disease-free.

• Skirt Management is cutting away the bottom leaves to reveal the fruit clusters for easier fertilization, insect control, and harvesting.

3. De-Flowering:

• Male Flowers: Male flowers appear first in some banana species. In parthenocarpic cultivars, where pollination is unnecessary, the male flowers are removed so that the plant's resources can go toward developing the fruit.

• Female Flowers: Pick a handful of female flowers for pollination and fruit development if pollination is needed for specific types. Reduce the amount of female flowers so that you just have to care for a reasonable number of fruit clusters.

4. Controlling Fake Stem Cells:

• Once fruiting is over, trim the top of the pseudostem (the trunk-like structure). New suckers are encouraged to grow, which aids in the next round of fruit production.

• After fruit has been harvested, the strongest sucker should be selected and saved for the following season's harvest. Suckers should be cut off so that just one plant grows in each pot.

5. Instruction and Help:

• Support the plants using supports or trellises if you live in a windy location or plan on harvesting a lot of fruit at once. The pseudostem and fruit clusters need to be supported by stakes pushed into the ground close to the plant's base.

• Tying: Using a soft material or thread, gently tie the pseudostem to the stake to keep it from bending or toppling over. As the plant develops, you will need to readjust the ties.

• For tall banana cultivars or when controlling plant height, tipping or bending the pseudostem can promote lateral development and lessen the likelihood of the plant toppling over.

6. Ratoon Administration:

• After the main plant has finished fruiting, it can send up additional shoots from its rhizome, a process known as ratooning. Let one or two ratoons mature, then get rid of the others. Fruit can be harvested repeatedly from the same plant using this method.

• It's worth noting that different banana varieties, environmental factors, and management objectives may call for different approaches to pruning and training. If you're not sure how to prune and train your banana trees, it's best to ask a local agricultural specialist, extension service, or seasoned banana producer for advice.

• Proper pruning and training procedures allow producers to maximize fruit yield, plant health, light exposure, air circulation, insect control, and disease management in banana growing.

CHAPTER SIX
Growth Of Flowers And Fruit

The flowering and maturation of banana fruits are two essential steps in the plant's life cycle that result in the harvest of delicious fruit. Here's a rundown of how bananas go from flower to fruit:

1. Flowering:

• When it comes to timing, different banana kinds can bloom anywhere from 9 to 14 months after planting, with the exact date depending on factors like latitude, humidity, and other environmental and cultural considerations.

• Banana plants form a sizable inflorescence, also called the flower stalk or bunch. The inflorescence begins its ascent at the base of the pseudostem and curves over at the top.

• The inflorescences of banana plants consist of both male and female flowers. The inflorescence is composed of male and female flowers, with the male blooms located higher up and the female flowers lower down.

• Many banana cultivars have parthenocarpic female flowers, which means fruit can form even in the absence of pollination. However, pollination is necessary for fruit set in some types. This can happen organically with the help of pollinators or artificially with a little help from a human.

2. Growth in Fruits:

• Fruit Set: The female flowers produce fruit after pollination (if necessary). When a flower is pollinated, its ovary expands to produce a cluster of tiny fruit fingers.

• Fruit Development: Fruits grow longer and larger as they mature. The plant's energy and nutrients come from the pseudostem and leaves, which are used exclusively for fruit production.

• Fruits require varying amounts of time to mature, depending on the variety. The fruits' colour changes from green to yellow, crimson, or other hues as they ripen.

• Collect the fruit when it has achieved an optimal maturity level for eating or selling. Bananas, for example, can be used in different ways depending on their maturity (either green for cooking or ripe for eating).

Contributing Variables To Flowering And Fruit Setting:

Environmental factors like as ideal temperatures, humidity levels, and amounts of light are crucial for successful flowering and fruit set. Bananas do best in the warm, humid environments of the tropics and subtropics.

Fruit growth depends critically on the availability of vital minerals, especially potassium. If you want your fruits to set and grow to their full potential, you need to fertilize and manage your nutrients properly.

• Water Management: Sufficient and steady water supply is crucial for fruit to mature. Fruit quality and size can suffer from water stress.

• Better quality and greater fruit can be expected from plants if they are healthy. Overall plant health and fruit growth are aided by effective pest and disease management and consistent monitoring.

• For improved fruit quality and longer storage life, bananas are often collected when still green, then matured in storage. Maintaining fruit quality after harvest relies heavily on post-harvest activities including storage and ripening methods.

Growers can improve banana output and quality by taking advantage of optimal cultural methods, ensuring optimal pollination (if necessary), and prudently allocating resources during the fruit's development from bloom to harvest.

CHAPTER SEVEN
Management During Harvest And After

Bananas' quality, freshness, and market value depend heavily on how they are harvested and cared for afterward. The main procedures are as follows:

1. Harvesting:

• Bananas should be harvested when they have reached the optimal maturity for their intended usage and market demands. Banana varieties and regional tastes can affect this step. Some typical steps are:

• The fruit is fully grown, but it retains its green colour. It's most common applications are in the kitchen and for fresh, off-the-plant eating.

• The fruit's colour changes as it ripens, signalling the end of the unripe stage. It might be consumed quickly or has a short storage life.

• Full Colour: The fruit is perfectly ripe and can be eaten right now. It won't last as long in storage.

• Harvesting Method: Cut the fruit bunch off the plant with a sharp knife or machete. For the sake of the fruit's safety, it's best to keep some of the pseudostem attached to the bunch.

2. Treatment After Harvesting:

• Bananas need to be sorted and graded once they have been harvested. Give them a grade that reflects the needs of the market. This ensures consistency and boosts the product's appeal to consumers.

• Cleaning: pick out and discard any dirty or broken fruit from the bunch. The fruit should be handled carefully to prevent bruising or damage.

• Bananas need to be packed in crates, boxes, or bags, depending on their intended transport method. Fruit that has been properly packaged can survive the ordeal of being shipped.

• Bananas can be stored and transported under a variety of conditions, depending on their final destination and the needs of the market.

• Bananas picked while they are mature green can be kept at 13-16 degrees Celsius (55-61 degrees Fahrenheit) in a cool, well-ventilated place to postpone ripening.

• Store bananas at room temperature after they reach the desired ripeness to preserve their flavour and texture.

3. Ripening:

• Bananas, thanks to the ethylene gas they produce, can ripen on their own at ambient temperature, a process known as "natural ripening." Put green bananas in a cool, dry place and they'll ripen at their own pace. Protect them from hot temperatures and direct sunshine.

• Bananas can be ripened more quickly via artificial means, such as ethylene generators or ripening chambers, which expose the fruit to ethylene gas. With this technique, ripening may be managed more precisely, leading to more consistent results.

4. Managed Quality:

• Keep an eye on the bananas as they ripen and in storage to make sure they are in good shape. Bananas can quickly become infected, therefore it's important to remove any rotten fruit as soon as possible.

• Temperature and Humidity Control: Keep things at the right temperature and humidity while they're being stored and ripened to cut down on quality loss, mould growth, and spoilage.

5. Transportation:

• Bananas bruise easily, which can hasten spoilage and lower quality, so take care when harvesting and packing them.

• To keep the fruit at an optimal temperature and lengthen its storage life, cold chain management requires that refrigerated vehicles or containers be used for long-distance travel.

Bananas' quality, market value, and consumer happiness can be improved with careful harvesting and post-harvest management. Adherence to these standards contributes to a successful banana production and marketing operation by reducing losses, increasing the fruit's shelf life, and preserving its sensory qualities.

Adding Value And Promotion In Marketing

Bananas have been successfully commercialized thanks in large part to marketing and value addition. Here are some essential factors to think about:

• The demand, preferences, and trends in the banana market can be better understood with some in-depth market research. Find markets for your fruit, whether wholesale, retail, export, or processing, and learn what specifications they have for size, quality, packaging, and timing of deliveries.

• Branding and Packaging Work together to create a unique and eye-catching package that will keep the fruit fresh and look great on store shelves. Think of using recyclable or compostable materials. Create a memorable brand name that communicates the superiority of your bananas.

• Strict quality control methods should be put in place during all phases of banana production, from planting to harvesting to storage. Keep an eye on characteristics like size, colour, texture, ripeness, and flavour to make sure your product is up to par with the market and customer expectations.

• Products With Added Value: Investigate Banana Processing Options That Could Increase Profits. Bananas are often processed into other foods with added value, such as banana chips, dried bananas, banana puree, jam, bread, and smoothies. You may increase the value of your banana harvest and increase your share of the market by diversifying your product line.

• Farmers' markets, CSA programs, on-farm sales, and internet marketplaces are all examples of direct marketing strategies to think about. By going straight to the source, in the form of the customer, direct marketing can boost profits and customer loyalty.

• Potential Export Markets Investigate the possibility of exporting bananas if you live in an area with ideal growing conditions for different types of bananas. Maintain compliance with phytosanitary regulations, export only to countries with similar quality standards, and network with trustworthy export businesses.

• Get together with other local banana farmers, agricultural groups, or cooperatives to advertise and promote locally grown bananas, negotiate bulk orders, pool resources, and increase market access.

• Spend money on advertising and public relations to get the word out about your bananas. Promote your business in a number of ways: online (through social media), in print (via local advertising), at events like trade shows and agricultural expos, and so on.

• Promotional materials, recipe demos, and workshops can help educate customers on the health advantages, adaptability, and one-of-a-kind characteristics of bananas. The many uses, inherent sweetness, and portability of bananas as a snack or ingredient should be highlighted.

• Differentiate your bananas in the market by highlighting their unique qualities or certifications. Organic and fair trade certifications, for instance, might pique the interest of shoppers with a concern for the planet and social justice. Highlight the use of sustainable farming methods, distinctive flavour profiles, or specialized kinds.

In order to construct a reputable and successful banana marketing operation, it is essential to establish strong relationships with buyers, maintain consistent quality, meet delivery dates, and provide good customer service. To be competitive, you must consistently evaluate market dynamics, consumer preferences, and industry trends and adjust your marketing plans accordingly.

CHAPTER EIGHT
Challenges And Sustainable Methods

To reduce negative effects on the environment, guarantee future productivity, and boost social and economic well-being, it is essential to use sustainable methods when growing bananas. But there are several obstacles to incorporating eco-friendly methods into the banana industry. The following is a summary of sustainable practices and the difficulties they present:

1. Modalities of Agroecology:

• To reduce the spread of pests and diseases and to boost soil quality, rotate your crops. However, it might be difficult to locate acceptable rotation crops in commercial banana farming, since bananas are the primary crop.

• Bananas can be intercropped with other plants to increase biodiversity, facilitate pest management, and make the most efficient use of available land. Competition for resources and the management of varied crop needs can be challenging, though.

2. Insect and pest control using IPM:

• Beneficial insects, predatory mites, and parasitic wasps are only some of the natural enemies that can be used in biological management. However, getting the correct number of helpful organisms and keeping them there can be difficult.

• Cultural Practices: Reduce pest and disease incidence by the use of sanitation, trimming, and appropriate spacing. However, the use of cultural methods alone might be challenging when dealing with pests and diseases like Fusarium wilt.

3. Soil and Water Conservation:

• To reduce water waste, it is best to employ efficient watering methods, such as drip or micro-sprinklers.

However, small-scale farmers may be put off by the high initial investment cost and the need for technical knowledge for installation and maintenance.

• Soil Conservation: Reduce soil erosion and boost soil fertility through activities like cover cropping, mulching, and erosion control. However, it can be difficult to put into practice due to a lack of suitable cover crop species and a lack of available labour.

4. Nutritional Administration:

• Fertilizers should be applied based on the results of a soil nutrient analysis to achieve a healthy balance between plant uptake and loss of nutrients. However, it might be difficult for small-scale farmers to acquire proper soil nutrient analyses and to determine optimum fertilizer application rates.

• Reduce your use of synthetic fertilizers by switching to organic ones like compost, manure, or biofertilizers. However, organic fertilizers can be expensive and hard to come by.

5. Difficulties in Society and the Economy:

• Working Conditions: In large-scale commercial banana farms, it can be difficult to provide fair salaries, safe working conditions, and labour rights for workers.

• Small-scale farmers may have trouble achieving certification and market access requirements due to a lack of funds, knowledge, and infrastructure.

• Low profit margins and unpredictable market prices make it difficult for farmers to implement sustainable practices.

6. Global Warming:

• Climate change may increase the prevalence and severity of pests and illnesses, calling for more stringent measures to be taken in terms of pest management.

• Banana output can be impacted by changes in rainfall patterns and an increase in the frequency of droughts.

• Hurricanes, storms, and floods can do a lot of damage to banana plants and halt output.

Farmers, researchers, legislators, and industry participants all need to work together to find solutions to these problems. The barriers to implementing sustainable methods in banana farming can be reduced by government support, investment in R&D, capacity building, and market incentives. Increasing the number of businesses that embrace sustainable practices can be aided by educating farmers on the topic.

Conclusion

Growing bananas is a major agricultural industry around the world. It is essential for the success of banana production to have a thorough understanding of all facets of banana agriculture, from planting material selection and preparation to post-harvest management.

Bananas are grown in a wide range of temperatures and are particularly picky about the soil they're planted in. The availability of fertile seedlings is ensured by means of reproduction and propagation, such as the use of suckers or tissue culture. Irrigation, fertilizer, and pest control are all essential components of effective field management that contribute to robust plant growth and maximum harvest output.

Pruning and training methods keep plants in good shape, allowing more light and air to reach the plant's growing medium and increasing its yield. Careful harvesting and post-harvest management procedures ensure the quality and market value of the fruit, which are dependent on the plant's ability to flower and generate fruit.

Banana farming can be successful in the long run with the right mix of sustainable methods, marketing techniques, and value addition. The environmental effect of banana production can be reduced by the use of sustainable methods such integrated pest management, water and soil management, and nutrient management.

Banana agriculture, however, faces obstacles such as labour conditions, market access, and the effects of climate change, all of which demand focus and concerted action.

Banana farmers may work toward a more prosperous, ecologically friendly, and socially responsible industry by adopting sustainable methods, overcoming obstacles, and remaining abreast of industry developments and market expectations.

THE END

Made in the USA
Coppell, TX
13 May 2024

32333151R00059